Egyptian Mythology for Kids

Enthralling Myths and Legends of Gods, Goddesses, and Mythological Creatures

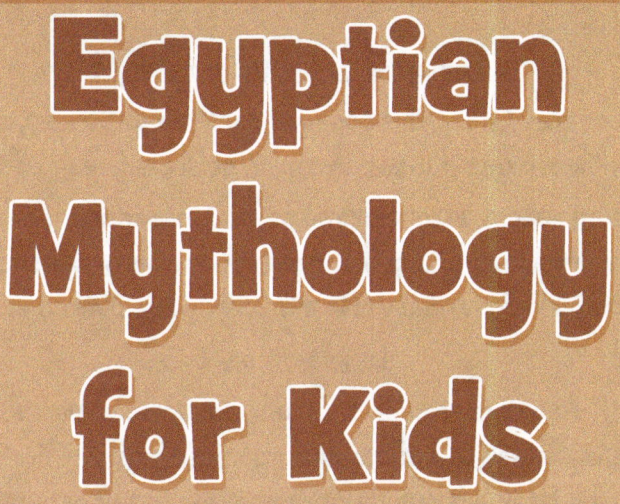

© Copyright 2023 - All rights reserved.

The content contained within this book may not be reproduced, duplicated, or transmitted without direct written permission from the author or the publisher.

Under no circumstances will any blame or legal responsibility be held against the publisher, or author, for any damages, reparation, or monetary loss due to the information contained within this book, either directly or indirectly.

Legal Notice:

This book is copyright protected. It is only for personal use. You cannot amend, distribute, sell, use, quote, or paraphrase any part, or the content within this book, without the consent of the author or publisher.

Disclaimer Notice:

Please note the information contained within this document is for educational and entertainment purposes only. All effort has been executed to present accurate, up-to-date, reliable, and complete information. No warranties of any kind are declared or implied. Readers acknowledge that the author is not engaging in the rendering of legal, financial, medical, or professional advice. The content within this book has been derived from various sources. Please consult a licensed professional before attempting any techniques outlined in this book.

By reading this document, the reader agrees that under no circumstances is the author responsible for any losses, direct or indirect, that are incurred as a result of the use of the information contained within this document, including, but not limited to, errors, omissions, or inaccuracies.

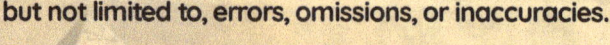

Table of Contents

Introduction	**1**
Chapter 1: The Origins of Egyptian Mythology	**2**
Chapter 2: Cosmology: When Everything Began	**11**
Chapter 3: The Reign of Ra	**20**
Chapter 4: The Story of Osiris	**27**
Chapter 5: The Journey of the Sun	**32**
Chapter 6: Afterlife Beliefs	**38**
Chapter 7: The Egyptian Pantheon	**46**
Chapter 8: Animal-Headed Gods	**54**
Chapter 9: The Sphinx	**65**
Chapter 10: Of Gods and Humans	**71**
Check out another book in the series	**78**
References	**79**

INTRODUCTION

When you hear the word "Egypt," what is the first thing that comes to mind? Chances are you think of mummies and pyramids. But the ancient Egyptians are also well known for their gods and goddesses.

Thousands of years ago, the Egyptians told creation stories. These myths helped the Egyptians make sense of the world around them. For example, they asked themselves, "Why does the sun rise every morning and set every evening?" or "What happens to the soul after a person dies?"

These stories helped them to understand where they came from and how they were supposed to live. Their myths told of mighty gods and goddesses who controlled the sun, the moon, and the stars.

Some of the gods were kind, although others were not. Read on and find out how Osiris became the Lord of the Dead. Who was Amun-Ra, the mightiest god of all? Why are statues of the jackal-headed Anubis found in tombs of the ancient pharaohs? Learn about the crocodile-headed Sobek and the Eye of Ra.

Learning about Egyptian mythology offers a fascinating glimpse into the beliefs of a people who learned how to thrive in the harsh desert. Their ancient tombs and temples have endured to this day, offering us a glimpse into their world.

Are you ready to learn all this and more? Then, let's get started!

Chapter 1: The Origins of Egyptian Mythology

What did the ancient Egyptians believe about their beginning? These stories offer an exciting glimpse into one of the oldest cultures in the world.

Like many other cultures, myths helped people to understand where they came from. These stories helped them make sense of things in their world. The ancient Egyptian people created stories that helped to explain events like how the world was created. These stories answered questions about who made the sun travel across the sky every day or why the moon and stars come out at night.

Myths helped them to understand nature. Why did the Nile River flood every year? What happened to people after they died? Who made their crops grow? What happened to people if they were bad or evil? These stories were told and retold for hundreds of years.

It is believed the ancient Egyptians were one of the oldest cultures in the world. Their origins date back to around 6000 BCE. They settled along the banks of the Nile River and began to grow crops and build villages.

The people of Egypt eventually formed two separate kingdoms. One was called Lower Egypt (to the north), and the other was Upper Egypt (to the south). The people of each kingdom had their own leaders, worshiped their own gods, and kept their own customs. They even had their own myths. Over time, they worshiped many of the same gods and believed in the same myths. They believed if they pleased the gods and their kings, they would have good lives.

Every Egyptian god had a purpose, from lifting the sun into the sky every morning to helping crops grow. Ancient Egyptian lives revolved around these beliefs. These stories also found their way into other cultures around the world, including the ancient Greeks and Romans.

Images of Egyptian gods and goddesses and myths have been found throughout Egypt. Some of these stories have been found painted on the walls of tombs. Others were written in stone or carved into temple walls. Some were written on **papyrus** *(pa-pie-rus)*, an ancient form of paper made from plants.

Images from the Book of the Dead on papyrus.
https://commons.wikimedia.org/wiki/File:Bookdead.jpg

Stone statues and carvings have been discovered in Egypt. Many of them are now in museums around the world. These ancient objects or **relics** *(rell-icks)* help to explain many beliefs of the ancient Egyptians and what they thought their gods and goddesses looked like.

Stone carving of Set and Horus adoring Ramesses.
https://commons.wikimedia.org/wiki/File:SethAndHorusAdoringRamsses_crop.jpg

Some statues are tiny, and others are over four hundred feet tall (a building over forty stories high)!

Carving of Nut.
https://www.metmuseum.org/art/collection/search/552609

Many images of Egyptian gods can still be seen in the burial chambers of unearthed tombs. They can be seen rising above the sands of great deserts.

Just as important to Egyptian civilization as the gods and goddesses that helped and protected them was water.

The Mighty Nile – The River of Life

The Nile River gave life to the Egyptians. Most of the vast lands of Egypt are desert, but the mighty river provided its people with enough water to grow crops and sustain life. Every year, rains came and caused the Nile River to flood. Too little rain meant that crops wouldn't grow. Too much flooding would ruin the crops and maybe even the people's homes. Who controlled the flooding? Well, the ancient Egyptians believed a god named **Hapi** *(hop-ee)* was responsible for the yearly flooding of the Nile.

> **Fun Fact**
> "The Nile River flows south to north. It is the longest river in the world at just over four thousand miles long!"

The ancient people living along the Nile River noticed that the Nile flooded year after year. They learned when it was time to plant and when to harvest. The people believed that otherworldly gods and goddesses were the reason for creating order in their world. They controlled things like birth, life, and death. These cycles repeated themselves over and over, just like the cycle of growing crops.

Every year, the Nile flooded, sending water over both banks and onto the land on either side. Much of the land was underwater for a few weeks. After that, the land was fertile and ready for planting. Much of Egypt beyond the river was nothing but sandy desert.

The Egyptians believed the river was a gift from the gods. Over many years, towns were built along the upper and lower banks of the Nile. The land was divided into two basic regions: Upper and Lower Egypt.

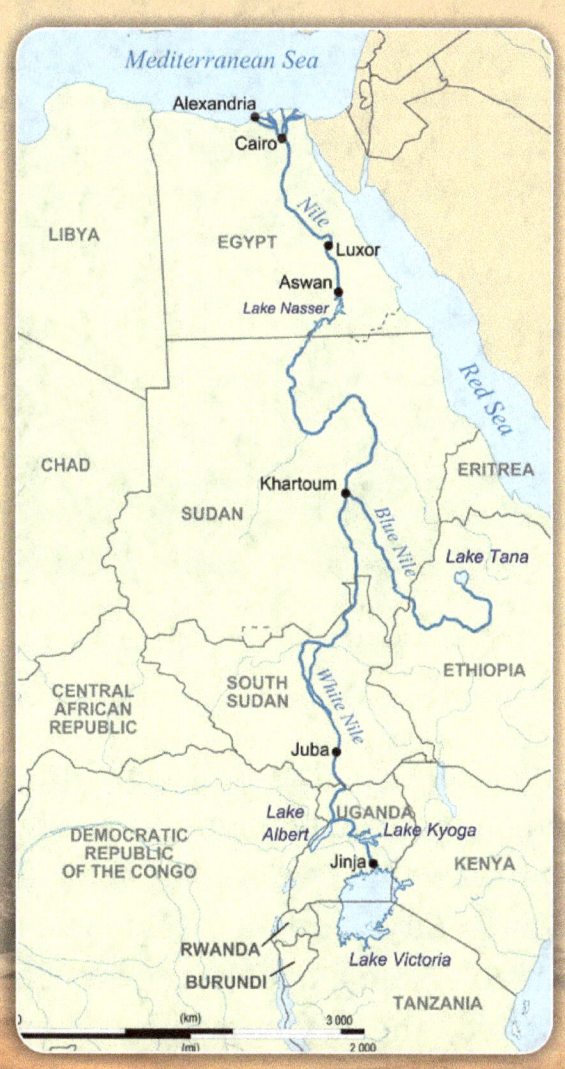

Route of the Nile River.
Hel-hama, CC BY-SA 3.0 <https://creativecommons.org/licenses/by-sa/3.0>, via Wikimedia Commons; https://commons.wikimedia.org/wiki/File:River_Nile_map.svg

Around 3100 BCE, a king of Upper Egypt named **Narmer** *(nar-mer)* unified Lower and Upper Egypt into one kingdom. He is also believed by historians to be the first **pharaoh** *(fair-oh)* of Egypt. He is also known as **Menes** *(men-ess)*.

Stone carving of Hapi, the river god, uniting Egypt.
Hedwig Storch, CC BY 3.0 <https://creativecommons.org/licenses/by/3.0>, via Wikimedia Commons; https://commons.wikimedia.org/wiki/File:Abu_Simbel_0219.JPG

Before Egypt was united, the kings of Upper and Lower Egypt wore different colored crowns. The crown of the king in Lower Egypt was red. The crown of the king of Upper Egypt was white. After the two regions of Egypt were united, the pharaoh wore a double crown. The lower half of the crown was red, and it was white on top. This united crown is often seen in paintings left behind by the ancient Egyptians.

Egyptian Myths and Rituals

Egyptian creation myths were created to help them to make sense of the world around them. They explained what happened to them after they died. Their stories explaining nature and the cycles of life were passed down from generation to generation.

The ancient Egyptians were taught how to honor their gods by priests who told their stories. Priests oversaw rituals to honor and remember them. The priests also took care of the temples.

Some myths gave direction to the later kings (also known as pharaohs) of Egypt and how they governed. This part of Egyptian life was known as the **myth of kingship**.

The ancient Egyptians firmly believed there was a real link between humans and the gods. That link was their pharaoh. The pharaohs were thought to be both human and godlike. As such, pharaohs were worshiped and respected.

Great monuments and statues were built to honor their pharaohs. When a pharaoh died, he was often buried in a great tomb. Some of them built pyramids, many of which survive today.

INTERESTING FACT

Only a pharaoh was allowed to make an offering to a god.

Chapter 1 Activity

Decide which of the following statements is true or false to gauge your understanding of this chapter and the origins of Egyptian mythology.

1. The Nile River flows north to south.

2. In ancient Egypt, everyone believed in and worshiped the same gods.

3. Writing or drawing on papyrus was the only method of telling myths and describing gods.

4. The Nile River was the most important river in ancient Egypt.

5. Osiris was the pharaoh who united Lower and Upper Egypt.

6. The myth of kingship said there was no link between the king of Egypt and the gods.

Chapter 1 Activity Answers

1. False. The Nile River flows from south to north.

2. False. The people of different regions in Egypt believed in and worshiped their own gods until Narmer united Upper and Lower Egypt.

3. False. The Egyptians painted or carved stories and images on tomb walls, built pyramids, and created statues.

4. True. The Nile River was essential for the planting and harvesting of crops.

5. False. Historians believe that Narmer was the first pharaoh and the one who united Egypt.

6. False. The ancient Egyptians believed the pharaoh was the living link between humans and the gods.

Chapter 2: Cosmology: When Everything Began

Cosmology *(kos-moll-o-gee)* is the study of the universe. In ancient times, most cultures around the world passed down their own myths or stories of how the universe was created.

Creation myths are called ***cosmogonies*** *(kos-mog-oh-nees)* or origin myths. Three major creation myths were told in ancient Egypt. Each had their own version of how the world and the universe came to exist.

Sometimes, details of the myths changed, such as the name of the god or goddess. Some of the stories were very similar. Each version depended on where they came from and in what era of Egyptian history they were told.

Some of the oldest myths come from **Hermopolis** *(herm-op-o-lis)*. Hermopolis was a city located near the boundary of Upper and Lower Egypt. People there worshiped eight gods known as the ***Ogdoad*** *(ogg-doh-d)*. These gods were paired: one male with one female.

According to their origin myth, in the beginning of time, nothing but water existed. This vast body of water was called **Nun** *(noon)*. Nun and his female equal, **Nunet** *(noon-et)*, were believed to live in every water particle, including the Nile River. **Kek** and his counterpart, **Keket** *(kek-et)*, became darkness. **Amun** *(ah-moon)* and his female equal, **Amunet** *(ah-mun-et)*, were "invisible" or hidden.

An explosion in the water caused a mound of dirt to rise up. From the mound of dirt rose **Atum** *(a-toom)*, the first god. Atum then made other gods and goddesses.

A temple relief representing the Ogdoad.
Dendera_Deckenrelief_02.JPG: Olaf Tauschderivative work: JMCC1 (talk)photographe/égyptologue, CC BY 3.0 <https://creativecommons.org/licenses/by/3.0>, via Wikimedia Commons; https://commons.wikimedia.org/wiki/File:L%27Ogdoade_d%27Hermopolis.jpg

The Ogdoad represented various aspects of nature, such as water, darkness, air or space, and things that were hidden or invisible.

The most well-known creation gods were worshiped at **Heliopolis** *(hell-ee-op-po-lis)*, a city located on the Nile Delta. The people of this region believed in and worshiped a group of nine gods known as the **Ennead** *(enn-ee-odd)*. These nine gods and goddesses included Atum, the sun god; Shu, the god of the air; and Osiris, the god of the dead. Another was Geb, the god of the earth. He was the god of harvests and made things grow, like fruits, vegetables, and grains.

Geb: Egyptian god of the earth.
Daniel Toye, CC BY-SA 3.0 <https://creativecommons.org/licenses/by-sa/3.0>,
via Wikimedia Commons; https://commons.wikimedia.org/wiki/File:Geb.svg

Fun Fact

> The Egyptians used art, images, and symbols to explain what a god or goddess did. For example, Geb is often depicted with a goose or bird on his head. The goose symbolized his gift of fertile land. He holds a scepter (sep-ter), implying power, in one hand and an ankh (aangk), a symbol of life, in the other.

Drawing of the Ennead on papyrus.
Buchsweiler, CC BY-SA 3.0 <https://creativecommons.org/licenses/by-sa/3.0>,
via Wikimedia Commons; https://commons.wikimedia.org/wiki/File:Enneade.jpg

In the Ennead's origin myth, only water existed at first. Then, Atum, the first god, emerged from the waters and floated upon it. He made himself into a mound of earth. He fathered children, **Shu** *(shoo)* and **Tefnut** *(teff-noot)*, who became the ancestors of other Egyptian gods.

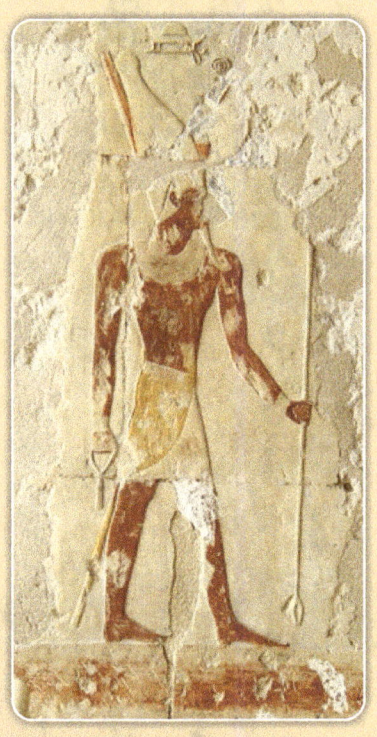

Stone relief of Atum.
jehouty, CC BY-SA 4.0 <https://creativecommons.org/licenses/by-sa/4.0>, via Wikimedia Commons; https://commons.wikimedia.org/wiki/File:Deir_el-Bahari_2016-03-25x.jpg

Another origin myth came from **Memphis** *(mem-fis)*, which later became the capital city of unified Egypt. Memphis was not far from Heliopolis. The people of Memphis worshiped **Ptah** *(puh-ta)*.

This origin story states Ptah existed before the Ennead and the rise of Atum from the waters. The world was created from Ptah's heart and tongue. When he spoke or described something, it was created.

Ptah is often drawn as a man wrapped in white cloth, much like a mummy. He holds a staff of power or authority, which also implies stability.

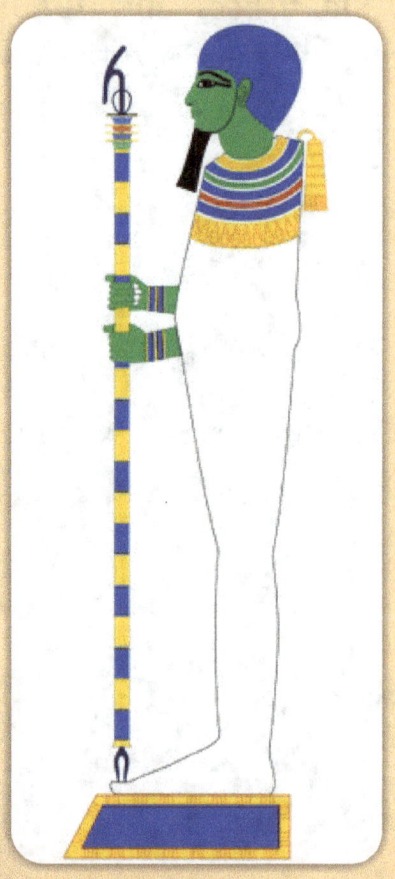

Ptah: A creator god from Memphis.
Jeff Dahl, CC BY-SA 4.0 <https://creativecommons.org/licenses/by-sa/4.0>,
via Wikimedia Commons; https://commons.wikimedia.org/wiki/File:Ptah_standing.svg

While creation myths were often similar, the origins and names of the gods and goddesses often differed. One thing these creation myths agreed upon was that the world (as a mound of earth) was borne of water or chaos. All the stories shared a mound of dirt rising out of the water. The story of the sun (the sun god Atum or Ra) rising from the mound was also shared among the creation myths.

Balance out of Chaos

During the creation of the world, harmony and balance were needed. So, the goddess of divine order was created. Her name was **Ma'at** *(muh-aht)*. She is often shown with a feather in her hair, which is the symbol of truth. She also holds an ankh. It was believed that when a person died, Ma'at would place her feather on a scale to determine if that person had lived honestly.

Image of Ma'at, the goddess of balance and truth.
No machine-readable author provided. Jeff Dahl assumed (based on copyright claims), CC BY-SA 4.0 <https://creativecommons.org/licenses/by-sa/4.0>, via Wikimedia Commons; https://commons.wikimedia.org/wiki/File:Maat.svg

Over the centuries, **rituals** *(rich-u-alls)* or ceremonies were created by priests to offer gifts and prayers to the gods and goddesses. This was very important when it came to the importance of Ma'at, who oversaw balance in the people's lives.

The sun god Ra rose every morning and traveled through the sky on his daily journey. **Nut**, the goddess of the night sky, covered the land when Ra completed his journey across the sky. The Nile River flooded every year. When one pharaoh died, another took his place.

Such events were part of the natural order. The ancient Egyptians believed this kind of order prevented chaos.

Time was also measured in the cycle of the four seasons: spring, summer, fall, and winter. The Egyptians also separated time by activities, such as when they planted and harvested their crops. For the ancient Egyptians, time was not measured by minutes or hours but by events or social functions.

Chapter 2 Activity

Correctly fill in the blanks in the following sentences.

1. The _____ was the name for the eight gods of Hermopolis.

2. At Heliopolis, _____ was known as the god of the earth.

3. The goddess of divine order or balance was called _____.

4. _____ was a god worshiped in Memphis.

5. In the creation myth of Hermopolis, the first god who emerged from the water was named _____.

6. The group of gods known as the Ennead consisted of _____ gods.

Chapter 2 Activity Answers

1. Ogdoad
2. Geb
3. Ma'at
4. Ptah
5. Atum
6. Nine

Chapter 3: The Reign of Ra

Over time, the gods and goddesses that were worshiped in different regions of Egypt blended together and formed one god. One of those gods was the sun god Atum. He became known as Atum-Ra and then simply **Ra** *(rah)*. The people considered him the first "king of the gods."

Image of Ra, the Egyptian sun god.
Jeff Dahl, CC BY-SA 4.0 <https://creativecommons.org/licenses/by-sa/4.0>, via Wikimedia Commons; https://commons.wikimedia.org/wiki/File:Re-Horakhty.svg

He was believed to have risen from the *primordial (pry-more-dee-al)* waters, meaning at the beginning of time. **Nun** symbolized the waters at the time of creation.

Nun raises the sun.
https://commons.wikimedia.org/wiki/File:Nun_Raises_the_Sun.jpg

After creating the world, the gods made Ra the first king of Egypt. He was powerful and magical. Images of Ra often show him with the head of a falcon or hawk and a large round disk on his head, symbolizing the sun.

Some believed that Ra was the sun, while others believed he had the *power* of the sun. The sun is vital for life, so he was one of the greatest gods in Egyptian mythology.

It was also believed that Ra created all life on the earth. Some believed that humans were formed from his sweat and tears.

He traveled through the sky every day in a boat. During the day, his journey across the sky was calm and peaceful. He always traveled from east to west.

As his day journey ended, he started his nighttime journey into the underworld or the world of the dead. It was not calm or peaceful.

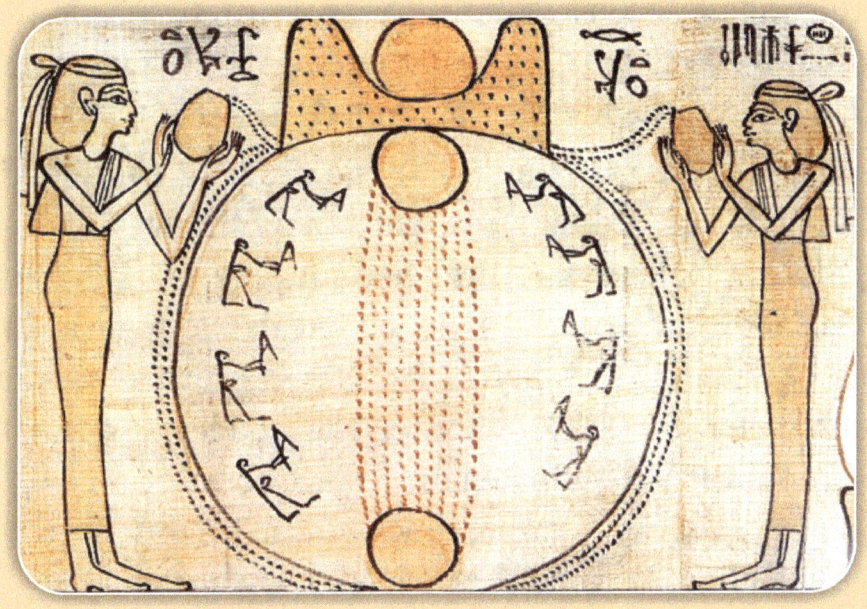

Image of sunrise at the creation.
https://commons.wikimedia.org/wiki/File:Sunrise_at_Creation.jpg

The Eye of Ra

In ancient Egypt, it was believed that the eyes of a god or goddess were filled with power. The same is true of Ra. The Eye of Ra is often symbolized by the large eye of a falcon. The symbol conveyed royal power, health, and

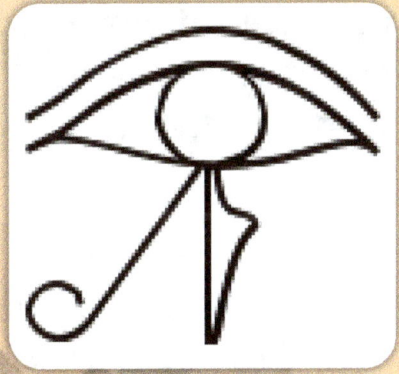

Eye of Ra.
https://commons.wikimedia.org/wiki/File:Abydos-Bold-hieroglyph-D10h.png

protection. In some myths, the Eye of Ra gave Ra the power to renew himself every morning at dawn as he emerged from the underworld.

The stories linked to the Eye of Ra took on different meanings. One of those myths was called the **Destruction of Mankind**. Experts are not sure when this myth was written. Some believe that it was written in the New Kingdom (c. 1539–1075 BCE). Others believe it was written much earlier in the Middle Kingdom (2030–1650).

In this myth, Ra grows angry at the growing evil found in humankind. The people no longer follow the way of Ma'at. They do not believe in truth, harmony, or good behavior. They disobey and ignore Ra. So, he decides to punish them. In one version of the myth, Ra asks the other gods and goddesses for advice. Ra chooses the goddess **Hathor** *(ha-ther)* to deliver the punishment. In the form of a cow, she was known as the wrathful Eye of Ra. In this form, she destroyed not only crops but people.

Many Egyptians died, but others survived. The story of the Destruction of Mankind is part of a longer, more complicated story that comes from the *Book of the Heavenly Cow*. In many Egyptian stories, the cow goddess is supported by the other gods and goddesses of the Ennead.

Fun Fact

> In ancient Egypt, the cow was greatly respected. Cows provided meat, hides, and milk. They pulled plows for farming and harvesting. Cows also symbolized fertility and motherhood.

Fun Fact

> The Book of the Heavenly Cow has been found in written form. It was even found in the tomb of the most famous mummy of all: Tutankhamun (toot-an-kah-moon). Other versions of the story have been found carved into the walls of several tombs.

Hathor.
Jeff Dahl, CC BY-SA 4.0 <https://creativecommons.org/licenses/by-sa/4.0>, via Wikimedia Commons; https://commons.wikimedia.org/wiki/File:Hathor.svg

Chapter 3 Activity

Choose the correct word to fill in the blanks.

1. The people of Egypt considered Ra the most powerful king of the gods, and he _____ (forgave/destroyed) the people when they became more evil.

2. The Eye of Ra takes the form of a _____ (snake/falcon).

3. Ra traveled through the sky every day in a _____ (boat/chariot).

4. Ra is the ancient Egyptian _____ (sun god/god of the air).

5. _____ (Anubis/Hathor) is known as the wrathful Eye of Ra.

Chapter 3 Activity Answers

1. The people of Egypt considered Ra the most powerful king of the gods, and he destroyed the people when they became more evil.

2. The Eye of Ra takes the form of a falcon.

3. Ra traveled through the sky every day in a boat.

4. Ra is the ancient Egyptian sun god.

5. Hathor is known as the wrathful Eye of Ra.

Chapter 4: The Story of Osiris

Osiris (*oh-sigh-rus*) is another well-known god in Egyptian mythology. He was the great-grandson of Ra. Known as the Lord of the Dead, he was the son of Geb (the earth god) and Nut (the goddess of the sky). He is mentioned in the *Book of the Dead* as a prince of not only the gods but also of man. He represented death and rebirth, which applied to nature and its seasons and the hope of an afterlife.

Osiris.
Jeff Dahl, CC BY-SA 4.0 <https://creativecommons.org/licenses/by-sa/4.0>, via Wikimedia Commons; https://commons.wikimedia.org/wiki/File:Standing_Osiris_edit1.svg

FUN FACT

"Osiris is one of the most well-known and popular gods of Egyptian mythology. Images of him show a handsome man wearing royal clothes. He was also known as the "Beautiful One" and the "Judge of the Dead.""

Osiris is often shown with the beard of a pharaoh and is wrapped like a mummy.

The myths tell of Osiris showing mankind how to give up their violent ways and learn how to grow crops instead. He gave them laws to live by. Osiris also taught humans how to be civil and polite.

Osiris had a brother named Seth. Seth was jealous of Osiris and killed him. He put his brother's body into a casket and tossed it into the Nile. Heartbroken, Osiris's wife **Isis** (*eye-sis*) searched for him. It was very important that she find his body so he could move into the afterlife. It took some time, but she finally found him.

When Seth heard that Isis had found the body, he sent some of his men to get it.

INTERESTING FACT

The ancient Egyptians believed that for the soul to move on after death the body had to be whole. This was why Isis searched so desperately for her husband after Seth killed him.

He then cut it up into pieces. He tossed the pieces back into the river and around the land of Egypt. Again, Isis searched for her dead husband.

Eventually, she found all of the pieces except one. She formed a piece of clay into the missing body part. The body of Osiris was made whole again. With the help of **Thoth** (*thow-th*), the moon god, and **Anubis** (*ah-new-bis*), the god of mummification, the pieces were wrapped inside cloths. Osiris then became the king of the dead. He is also known as the god of the underworld.

Osiris and Isis had a son named **Horus** *(hore-us)*. He should have taken the place of Osiris, but Seth made himself the king of Egypt after Osiris died. When Horus grew older, he wanted revenge against his uncle. Seth wanted to kill Horus since he didn't want his nephew to take his throne.

For many years, the two fought each other. One time, Horus lost an eye. Another time, Seth was wounded. Once, they both took on the form of a hippopotamus, and each tried to drown the other in the Nile River. Their fights always ended in a tie.

Finally, Horus won. He took back the throne of Egypt, and he banished his uncle from Egypt. Horus was the last divine god to rule Egypt. After him, human pharaohs ruled the land.

Stone carving of the fight between Horus and Seth.
I, Rémih, CC BY-SA 3.0 <http://creativecommons.org/licenses/by-sa/3.0/>, via Wikimedia Commons; https://commons.wikimedia.org/wiki/File:Edfu47.JPG

Chapter 4 Activity

Choose the correct answer to the multiple-choice questions below.

1. After Osiris died, he became _____.
   a. Part of the night sky
   b. The Lord of the Dead
   c. The Peacekeeper
2. After Seth killed Osiris, this goddess went looking for him:
   a. Nut
   b. Isis
   c. Anubis
3. When Seth and Horus fought, they both took the form of a.
   a. Snake
   b. Falcon
   c. Hippopotamus
   d. Crocodile
4. Horus was known as _____.
   a. The god of the earth
   b. The god of war
   c. The god of the sky
   d. The god of the Nile

Chapter 4 Activity Answers

1. B – The Lord of the Dead
2. B – Isis
3. C – Hippopotamus
4. C – The god of the sky

Chapter 5: The Journey of the Sun

Ra was the sun god. People, the land, and animals need sunlight for life. So, Ra's power had an effect on all living things. His main job was to travel across the sky every day to give heat and light to the world.

The ancient Egyptians believed the sun rose out of the water every morning and then returned to it every evening. They tried to understand why the sun didn't fizzle out!

Every evening, Ra's boat would reach the western horizon, and the sun would disappear. Ra sank into the waters of the underworld, bringing night to the world.

The underworld was known as the **Duat** *(doo-at)*. The underworld was also a place filled with monsters. Strange creatures lived in the caves and darkness of the underworld. Imagine a jackal with many heads or flaming snakes!

As Ra traveled through the underworld, it was believed that he could restore life to the dead while he was there. That way, the souls could experience some enjoyment in their afterlife.

On his journey through the Duat, Ra was joined by a crew of men who pulled his boat through the darkest of night and the waters of the underworld. In some versions of the myth, Ra is joined by Thoth, the god of wisdom, and Ma'at, the goddess of justice, truth, and balance.

> **FUN FACT**
> "Ra's journey through the day and night symbolized the cycle of life, from birth to death to rebirth."

Some of these stories about Ra were written in **hieroglyphs** *(hi-row-glifs)*, which were pictures or symbols. They were carved on the walls of tombs and written on sheets of papyrus. One collection of stories and magic spells is found in the Book of Gates.

The **Book of Gates** tells the story of what happens to Ra in the underworld during each of the twelve hours of the night. Different versions of the Book of Gates were told. In one version, twelve separate gates are described. Ra had to pass through one gate for every one of the twelve hours of the night. Behind those gates were serpents and other dangers that Ra had to face.

Ra in the underworld.
https://commons.wikimedia.org/wiki/File:Book_of_Gates_Barque_of_Ra_cropped.jpg

Ra had to overcome each danger before he could reemerge at dawn the following morning. The second gate was guarded by the "Swallower of Sinners." Behind the gate was a lake of fire.

Behind the tenth gate was Ra's fiercest enemy: the serpent god **Apophis** *(a-poe-fiss)* or **Apep** *(a-pep)*. Apophis was also known as the "Great Serpent" and the god of chaos. Every night, Apophis would attack Ra. The giant snake would try to stare at Ra and cast him under his spell.

Other gods living in the underworld tried to help Ra by throwing a net over the snake. They then tied Apophis up and cut him into pieces. Every night, Ra won his victory over Apophis. He returned to the land of the living and once again made his journey across the sky. For one more day, order was restored.

Some versions of Ra's journey tell of Osiris sitting in his judgment hall in the underworld. In front of Osiris is a set of scales. A dead person's heart is weighed against a feather on these scales. The results decide if a deceased soul will have a happy afterlife or a miserable one.

Some versions of the story say that while Ra was in the underworld, he blended with Osiris, the god of the dead. Other versions tell of Osiris and Ra fighting together.

Image from Book of Caverns.
https://commons.wikimedia.org/wiki/File:Book_of_caverns_(KV9)_fifth_division.jpg

The Book of Caverns also tells of Ra's journey at night. This book divided the underworld

> **Fun FACT**
>
> " A full version of the Book of Caverns was found in the tomb of Ramesses VI in the Valley of the Kings. This valley is known to be the cemetery for New Kingdom pharaohs. "

into six parts. In each of these six parts, Ra had to defeat a variety of gods and goddesses.

At the end of the journey, just before dawn, Ra took the form of a **scarab** (*scare-ub*) beetle. In ancient Egypt, the scarab beetle was a sacred religious symbol of renewal or transformation. The scarab beetle rolled the disk of the sun before him as he moved toward the eastern horizon. There, he appeared as Ra and repeated his journey across the sky, bringing warmth and light once again.

Ra in his boat.
https://commons.wikimedia.org/wiki/File:Ra_Barque.jpg

Chapter 5 Activity

Find and circle the words found in the list below.

s	l	a	t	t	o	m	b	s	d	o	s
o	s	t	b	b	k	e	i	o	u	q	e
u	c	w	i	i	y	t	j	l	a	d	r
l	a	j	b	b	g	s	b	y	t	a	p
s	r	r	a	a	a	p	t	m	e	y	e
s	a	l	l	l	p	n	e	t	b	t	n
k	b	g	a	a	p	o	p	h	i	s	t
m	f	o	n	n	k	f	s	e	n	m	s
q	n	r	c	c	m	d	a	r	u	e	k
u	n	d	e	e	r	w	o	r	l	d	s

- Ra
- underworld
- Duat
- souls
- balance
- tombs
- serpent
- Apophis
- scarab

Chapter 5 Activity Answers

s	l	a	t	o	m	b	s	d	o	s
o	s	t	b	k	e	i	o	u	q	e
u	c	w	i	y	t	j	l	a	d	r
l	a	j	b	g	s	b	y	t	a	p
s	r	r	a	a	p	t	m	e	y	e
s	a	l	l	p	n	e	t	b	t	n
k	b	g	a	p	o	p	h	i	s	t
m	f	o	n	k	f	s	e	n	m	s
q	n	r	c	m	d	a	r	u	e	k
u	n	d	e	r	w	o	r	l	d	s

Chapter 6: Afterlife Beliefs

Ancient Egyptians believed that a person's soul continued to live after death. Their myths were an important way for them to determine what happened to a person after they died and what they might expect afterward. Numerous stories of the afterlife can be found in ancient writings and images in tombs.

One of the most common beliefs was that people would be judged after death. Was the person good or not? Did they deserve to have a happy afterlife? Or would their soul travel on through eternity or be tortured and destroyed?

The answers to such questions are found in ancient Egyptian *funerary* (fee-un-r-rare-ee) texts. These texts changed over the centuries. In the Old Kingdom, the **Pyramid Texts** say the afterlife was meant only for the kings. As such, the Pyramid Texts, which were actually magic spells, were often found carved into the walls of kings' tombs after they died.

Portion of the Pyramid Texts in a pyramid.
https://commons.wikimedia.org/wiki/File:Unas_Pyramidentexte.jpg

In the Middle Kingdom, the **Coffin Texts** were written. The Coffin Texts were also magic spells, but they could be found on the coffin of anyone who could afford it. These texts closely followed much of what had been found in the Pyramid Texts.

In the New Kingdom, the **Book of the Dead**, the most well-known Egyptian funerary text, became popular. The collection of spells in the *Book of the Dead* focuses on the afterlife and what would happen when a person died.

Fun Fact

> The Book of the Dead was not a single book of magic spells written by one person. It was a collection of writings that were written over the centuries by different people. The texts were given the name Book of the Dead because they were found in tombs.

The *Book of the Dead* was a blend of the Pyramid and Coffin Texts. It contained a large number of the same spells that had been written in the Pyramid and Coffin Texts. These spells were written on papyrus by scribes and then buried with the mummy in its tomb.

But what did these texts say? Why were they important? They gave instructions for how the dead should behave in the afterlife. They also told the dead person how to restore their body or make it work in the afterlife.

The *Book of the Dead* has four parts. Each part offers tips for the departed soul. It talks about the following:

- How to protect the body when it was in the tomb;

- How to make the long journey into the underworld;
- How to pass the judgment of the gods in the underworld;
- How they might exist in the next world.

Another version of the afterlife included Osiris. After death, the soul appeared before Osiris, the god of the dead and the lord of the underworld. He and other judges would determine if the person had lived a good life.

In many versions, the soul of the person who lived a good life would continue to do what they had done in life. So, a man who made a living as a farmer before he died would be a farmer after he died, but he would not be sad or worried.

To determine whether a person was deserving of the afterlife, Osiris would weigh a dead human's soul in a process known as the Weighing of the Heart. Later versions of this myth included **Anubis**, guardian of the scales. **Ammit** (*am-mit*), a creature of the underworld with the head of a crocodile, would be waiting close by. If the soul was not worthy, Ammit would swallow the person's heart. The god of judgment or wisdom, **Thoth**, would record the results.

Image of Osiris judging the dead.
https://commons.wikimedia.org/wiki/File:Osiris,_God_of_the_Dead.jpg

Another version of the Weighing of the Heart had Anubis doing the judging. He would hold a feather in his hand (representing Ma'at, the goddess of justice). A heart that weighed more than the feather was deemed unworthy of an afterlife and fed to Ammit.

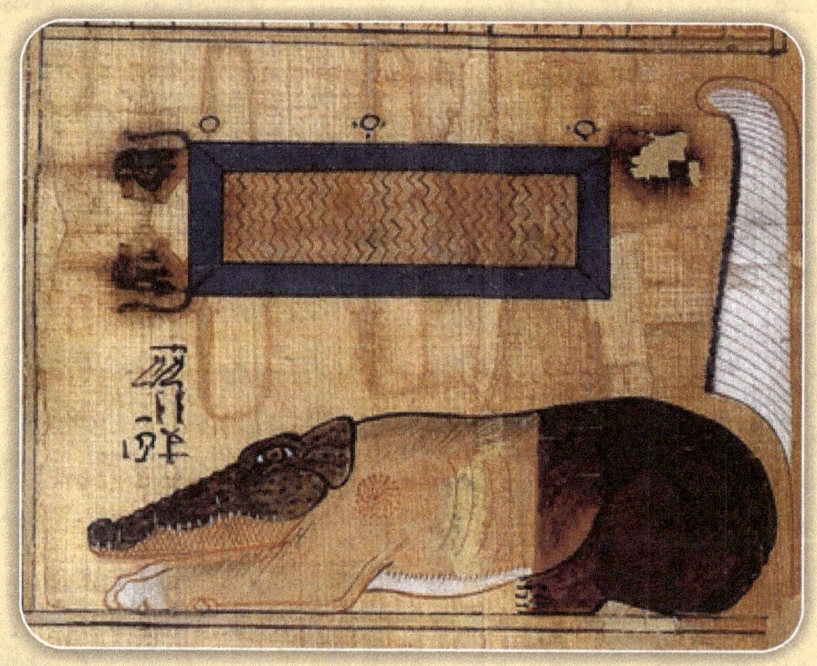

Image of Ammit.
https://commons.wikimedia.org/wiki/File:Early_Ammit.jpg

Ammit had the head of a crocodile and the upper body of a lion. Her hind part looked like a hippopotamus. The image of these three deadly animals implied that the bad person's soul would never escape its fate.

Did commoners take the same journey through the underworld as pharaohs? Some writings say they did. In the Coffin Texts, it is implied that as long as spells were carved into the dead person's coffin, they would be protected. These spells would also give the person magic to move into the afterlife.

The *Book of the Dead* also contains spells that were used by everyone on their journey into the afterlife. The spells contained within the *Book of the Dead* provided protection, knowledge, and guidance to the dead as they made their way through the underworld.

In the afterlife, it was believed that a person might be called upon to work in the fields. Grains like wheat and barley were very important to the Egyptians. These grains were needed to make bread, which fed the people.

Fun Fact: Wheat and barley were believed to be vital food for the dead.

Image of the Field of Reeds on papyrus.
https://commons.wikimedia.org/wiki/File:BD_Field_of_Hotep.jpg

Since most people in ancient Egypt worked in the fields and farmed, they were expected to work in and harvest the fields after death in the **Field of Reeds**. The Field of Reeds was paradise. One of the first mentions of the Field of Reeds was in the Pyramid Texts, but it is later mentioned in the Coffin Texts and the *Book of the Dead*.

Other myths suggest that after a soul completed its journey through the underworld and was deemed worthy of an afterlife, the person would be given a plot of land. In this way, they were assured that their life would continue in the afterlife much as it had in their real life.

Chapter 6 Activity

Which of the following questions are true and which are false?

1. The Egyptians believed that the body and the soul were gone forever once a person died.//
2. The Field of Reeds was a pasture that a soul had to pass through on foot.
3. The head of Ammit was a scarab beetle.
4. The Book of the Dead has four parts.
5. Writings from the Pyramid and Coffin Texts can still be seen on tomb walls.

Chapter 6 Activity Answers

1. False
2. False
3. False
4. True
5. True

Chapter 7: The Egyptian Pantheon

The people of ancient Egypt worshiped many gods and goddesses. In fact, over the centuries, it is believed that more than two thousand gods were worshipped! Each god or goddess had a purpose. Ra was the sun god. He gave people warmth and light. Seth was the god of storms and chaos.

A **pantheon** *(pan-thee-on)* is a group of gods and goddesses. Some of the gods aren't as well known, although they still played an important role in Egyptian society. Let's explore some of the most famous gods and goddesses of ancient Egypt.

Amun-Ra —During the years of the New Kingdom, **Amun** was seen as one of the most powerful gods. He was believed to have created the universe and all life. Amun was known as the "god of all gods" throughout Egypt, especially along the banks of the Nile River.

Image if Amun-Ra.
FDRMRZUSA, CC BY-SA 4.0 <https://creativecommons.org/licenses/by-sa/4.0>, via Wikimedia Commons; https://commons.wikimedia.org/wiki/File:Amun-Ra.svg

Ra was the god of the sun and light. He made the journey through the sky every day and then traveled through the underworld every night.

Over the centuries, the powers of these two gods (Amun and Ra) became known by a single name: **Amun-Ra**.

In images of Amun-Ra, he holds a scepter (symbolizing power or authority) and an ankh (symbolizing life).

Osiris – **Osiris** (*oh-sigh-rus*) was the god of the dead and the god of the underworld. He was worshiped for his power over death and the afterlife. Yet he was also honored and respected for his power over the Nile River and its yearly flooding. This yearly flooding was very important for the growing of crops on both sides of the river.

> **FUN FACT**
> The Egyptian pharaohs believed they were the manifestation of the sun god Ra and held his power. They were believed to be the human link between man and the gods.

Stone carving of the head of Osiris.
https://commons.wikimedia.org/wiki/File:Head_of_the_God_Osiris,_ca._595-525_B.C.E..jpg

Osiris was the husband of Isis. He was also the son of the earth god Geb and the sky goddess Nut. In early Egyptian history, Osiris was believed to have shown the people how to raise and grow crops. Due to his kindness, he was also known as the eternal good being.

However, because the people admired him so much, his brother, Seth, became very jealous of him. Seth killed Osiris. After Osiris died, he became the god of the underworld. There, he judged the dead. He did this by weighing their heart to determine if they had been good in life. If they were, their soul would live on. If not, their soul was eaten by a monster.

Image of Nephthys.
Jeff Dahl, CC BY-SA 4.0 <https://creativecommons.org/licenses/by-sa/4.0>, via Wikimedia Commons; https://commons.wikimedia.org/wiki/File:Nepthys.svg

Nephthys – **Nephthys** *(nef-this)* was the sister of Isis. She was known to protect the souls of the dead on their journey to the underworld, including the pharaohs. She and her sister Isis became known as the goddesses who protected mummies and **canopic** *(can-op-pic)* jars. These jars were special containers used during the **mummification** *(mum-if-a-kay-shon)* process. One part of the process was to wrap the dead body in strips of cloth. The canopic jars held the vital organs of the dead, which they would need in the afterlife.

Nephthys is often shown wearing a symbol of a door with a basket on top of that door. The images are believed to imply her name as "Lady of the Temple." She was known as a helpful goddess who offered protection and assistance for those who mourned or grieved over a dead loved one.

Hathor – Hathor *(ha-ther)* was loved by the people of both Upper and Lower Egypt as a mother figure. She was also known as the god of beauty. Hathor was one of the oldest gods in the Egyptian pantheon. So, why is she often shown wearing cow horns?

Cows were greatly respected in Egypt. They helped prepare the ground for planting and harvesting. Cows also provided nourishment or food for the people. Like the cow, Hathor was a goddess known to provide support and security for the people.

Image of Hathor.
Jeff Dahl, CC BY-SA 4.0 <https://creativecommons.org/licenses/by-sa/4.0>, via Wikimedia Commons; https://commons.wikimedia.org/wiki/File:Hathor.svg

Isis – **Isis** *(eye-sis)* is one of the most famous goddesses in the Egyptian pantheon. She is often shown wearing a throne atop her head, which symbolizes stability. She was also thought of as the divine mother of the pharaohs who ruled over Egypt.

Isis was the goddess of healing and magic. She represented goodness and femininity. Isis was married to Osiris. After Osiris's brother killed him, she searched for his body for a long time. When she found him, she prepared his body for his burial. Her sister, Nephthys, helped her.

Isis became known as the goddess who protected mummies. She was also known to protect the kings of Egypt. She had many other names, such as the "Mistress of the Heavens" or "The Great Magic."

Every one of the gods and goddesses of ancient Egypt had a purpose. Perhaps that is why there were thousands of them! Among those gods and goddesses were those that looked half-human and half-animal, like Ra. Why? Let's explore those gods and goddesses in the next chapter.

Chapter 7 Activity

Choose the correct answer to the multiple-choice questions below.

1. Isis was married to _____.
    a. Ra
    b. Amun
    c. Osiris
    d. Seth
2. Hathor wore _____ on her head
    a. An image of a snake in a circle
    b. An image of a doorway
    c. An image of a pigeon
    d. An image of the sun with horns
3. A pantheon is _____.
    a. A group of houses
    b. A group of gods
    c. A temple where the gods were worshiped.
    d. None of the above
4. This image symbolized life.
    a. A scepter
    b. A staff
    c. An ankh
    d. A scarab beetle
5. This goddess helped to prepare the dead for their journey into the afterlife.
    a. Nephthys
    b. Hathor
    c. Ma'at
    d. Tefnut

Chapter 7 Activity Answers

1. C – Osiris
2. D – Image of the sun with horns
3. B – A group of gods
4. C – ankh
5. A - Nephthys

Chapter 8: Animal-Headed Gods

A number of gods and goddesses in the Egyptian pantheon were often depicted with animal heads, like Ra, who had a falcon head. Why did some gods and goddesses have animal heads and human bodies? Why did some gods have bodies with different animal parts?

Often, the animal head was used as a symbol of a god's power. The head or body of an animal was used to represent the power of that god.

Take Ra, for example. He had the head of a falcon. What did that mean to the ancient Egyptians? The falcon was a hunting bird. It had the power to fly high in the sky and look down upon the land. As such, the falcon was linked to power and majesty.

The human form of a god might also be linked to a particular animal based on their personality. In other words, a god or goddess could be known as a *shape-shifter* (a human or animal that could change its shape and abilities.)

Let's explore a few of these animal-headed gods.

Anubis: The God of Mummification

One of the most famous animal-headed gods of the Egyptians was **Anubis** *(ah-new-bis)*. He is often portrayed with the head of a jackal. In a way, a jackal is like a wolf. Jackals were sacred to the ancient Egyptians. They are fierce and protective animals.

Anubis was often known as a protector of tombs or burial sites. His head is painted black to represent the darkness of death.

Anubis is closely linked to cemeteries and burial grounds. His primary job was to guard the dead. The legend of Anubis says that he helped to wrap the body of his father Osiris after his uncle Seth killed him and tossed his body into the Nile River.

Image of Anubis.
Jeff Dahl, CC BY-SA 4.0 <https://creativecommons.org/licenses/by-sa/4.0>, via Wikimedia Commons; https://commons.wikimedia.org/wiki/File:Anubis_standing.svg

Anubis had several important jobs. He helped Isis prepare Osiris for burial in a process known as ***embalmment*** (*em-ball-ment*). This process preserved the body of a dead person and turned them into mummies. The Egyptians believed the mummy held the spirit or soul of a dead person. Anubis guarded the tombs where mummies were buried.

INTERESTING FACT

- In ancient Egypt priests who prepared the dead for their journey through the underworld wore the mask of a jackal.
- The Egyptians believed that if a body was preserved in death as it was in life (if they were mummified) the body would last forever in the afterlife.

Horus - Lord of the Sky

Horus *(hore-us)* was the son of Osiris and Isis. He is often known as Horus the Younger or the falcon god and the sky god. Horus had a lot of responsibilities. He was known to protect the royal family.

Image of Horus.
Jeff Dahl, CC BY-SA 4.0 <https://creativecommons.org/licenses/by-sa/4.0>, via Wikimedia Commons; https://commons.wikimedia.org/wiki/File:Horus_standing.svg

Horus was often symbolized as a falcon with a double crown on his head, symbolizing the unification of Lower and Upper Egypt, as well as kingship.

Horus was told by Isis, his mother, to protect the people of Egypt against Seth, his uncle who had killed his father. Seth wanted to become the king of Egypt, but he was not a good man. He and Horus fought often. Horus finally won and took his father's place as king.

Horus was known to guide the souls of the dead into the underworld, where they were judged by his father, Osiris.

Seth: The God of Evil and Chaos

In ancient Egypt, some animal heads were not really an animal at all. Instead, these forms could be a creature not known to mankind. These are known as "Seth animals." Seth animals were believed to exist in ancient Egyptian mythology but have no relation in nature.

Image of Set.
Jeff Dahl (talk · contribs), CC BY-SA 4.0 <https://creativecommons.org/licenses/by-sa/4.0>, via Wikimedia Commons; https://commons.wikimedia.org/wiki/File:Set.svg

The Seth animal is often seen in Egyptian art as a mythical animal or even a monster. One of these monsters was used to depict the image of Seth, also spelled as Set.

Seth was the son of Geb and Nut. He was known as the god of storms, chaos, and destruction. Because of his ability to cause chaos, evil, and darkness, he was greatly feared and hated by many. However, he provided a balance between good and evil, so he was accepted by some.

In one myth, he transformed into Apophis, the giant snake that tried every night to stop Ra from leaving the underworld. In another story, Seth protected Ra from the attacks of Apophis, the great serpent snake.

Bastet: The Cat Goddess

The ancient Egyptians respected and honored cats. Why? Well, they got rid of mice, snakes, and other pests that could damage their crops. Cats were also believed to protect the pharaohs. The ancient Egyptians thought cats were magical creatures and could bring good luck.

Image of Bastet.
FDRMRZUSA, CC BY-SA 4.0 <https://creativecommons.org/licenses/by-sa/4.0>, via Wikimedia Commons; https://commons.wikimedia.org/wiki/File:Bastet_mirror.svg

Bastet *(ba-stet)* was worshiped as the cat goddess. She was believed to have been as fierce as a lion. Yet, Bastet was also believed to have a soft or gentle nature.

Bastet is often shown holding a **sistrum**, a sacred musical instrument in ancient Egypt. A sistrum is similar to a rattle. This item was used during religious ceremonies and some dances. She is also shown holding an ankh, the symbol of power.

Bastet was believed to have a warrior-like side to her personality. This side was known as **Sekhmet** *(sek-met)*. Sekhmet was believed to contain the power of the Eye of Ra. She is often shown with the head of a lion. On her head is the symbol of Ra (the sun). A deadly cobra snake is wrapped around the sun.

> **FUN FACT**
> " Egyptians believed that cats were magical and brought good luck. People often gifted cats with jewels and treated them like royalty! "

Like Amun-Ra, Bastet and Sekhmet merged into one goddess.

Image of Sekhmet.
Eternal Space, CC BY-SA 4.0 <https://creativecommons.org/licenses/by-sa/4.0>, via Wikimedia Commons; https://commons.wikimedia.org/wiki/File:Sekhmet_(Goddess).png

Sobek: The Crocodile God

In some regions of ancient Egypt, crocodiles were greatly admired. **Sobek**, the crocodile god, is often shown with the head of a crocodile. He is considered one of the *minor* (not as important) gods of the ancient Egyptians.

Even so, he was believed to have a close relationship with Ra. One myth states that Sobek, due to his nature as a meat lover, could not resist eating some of Osiris when his body was thrown into the Nile River.

Because Sobek had eaten the pieces out of hunger and not anger, his tongue was cut out. Egyptians believed this was why the crocodile has no tongue.

Image of Sobek.
Jeff Dahl, CC BY-SA 4.0 <https://creativecommons.org/licenses/by-sa/4.0>, via Wikimedia Commons; https://commons.wikimedia.org/wiki/File:Sobek.svg

Fun Fact

> Crocodiles actually do have a tongue, but it doesn't move. It is attached to the bottom of their mouth. Since they spend so much time underwater, their tongue helps to keep their throat closed. They do not need their tongue to swallow food, but they do use it to regulate their body heat!

In parts of ancient Egypt, crocodiles were considered creatures of great strength and power. As such, Sobek was believed to protect the Egyptian armies and the pharaohs. Some pharaohs kept pits of crocodiles near their temples. Sometimes, the animals were killed and mummified to provide food for the pharaohs in the afterlife.

Tefnut: The Goddess of Moisture

Tefnut was known as the goddess of moisture or rain. Of course, water is life-giving and is important for growing crops. Tefnut is often shown with the head of a lion. She is also seen with the sun disk on her head, but she has *two* cobra heads on either side rather than just one like Bastet wears.

Tefnut was known as a high priestess, but she was mainly known as the water goddess who made the crops grow. It was said that when she cried, her tears fell to Earth and watered the land.

In one myth, Tefnut was believed to help her mother Nut hold up the sky. But Tefnut had an angry side. That was when her lion face appeared. Another myth tells how Tefnut roamed through the desert after her father Ra punished the people of Egypt for being disobedient.

In ancient Egypt, the gods and goddesses with animal heads were believed to share a link with the nature of a certain animal. A number of animals found in Egypt were given great respect. Some of these animals were the cat, the hippopotamus, the crocodile, and the scarab beetle.

Image of Tefnut.
A8takashi, CC BY-SA 4.0 <https://creativecommons.org/licenses/by-sa/4.0>, via Wikimedia Commons; https://commons.wikimedia.org/wiki/File:Tefnut.png

Chapter 8 Activity

Draw a line to match the animal head to the correct god or goddess.

Jackal head • • Horus

Crocodile head • • Bastet

Cat head • • Seth/Set

"Monster head" • • Sobek

Falcon with crown head • • Anubis

Chapter 8 Activity Answers

Jackal head – Anubis

Crocodile head – Sobek

Cat head – Bastet

"Monster head" – Seth or Set

Falcon with crown - Horus

Chapter 9: The Sphinx

Perhaps one of the most recognizable images of Egypt is the **Great Sphinx** *(ss-finks)*. The sphinx is a mythical creature believed to act as a protector or guardian. The sphinx has the body of a lion and the face of a human. Many sphinxes were built in Egypt, but the Great Sphinx is the most famous of them all. The Great Sphinx can be found at Giza.

Image of the Sphinx and one of the pyramids of Giza.
Hesham Ebaid, CC0, via Wikimedia Commons;
https://commons.wikimedia.org/wiki/File:Sphinx_with_the_third_pyramid.jpg

Who built the Great Sphinx, and why? The Great Sphinx was carved into a rock outcropping to protect the tomb of Pharaoh Khafre against thieves. The face of the Sphinx is believed by many to be of Khafre (c. 2575–2465 BCE). Some historians disagree. Others believe that the head of the Great Sphinx depicted an Egyptian god.

In Egypt, the head of a sphinx was often male, signifying strength, ferocity, and royal power. Sphinxes were believed to be able to revive the pharaoh's soul by taking on the power of the sun and other gods.

Some sphinxes found in ancient Egypt have female faces. One such sphinx has the face of Pharaoh **Hatshepsut** *(haat-shep-soot)*. She was a famous ruler who brought many riches and works of art to Egypt through trade.

Statue of Pharaoh Hatshepsut.
Keith Schengili-Roberts, CC BY-SA 2.5 <https://creativecommons.org/licenses/by-sa/2.5>, via Wikimedia Commons; https://commons.wikimedia.org/wiki/File:Hatshepsut-CollosalGraniteSphinx01_MetropolitanMuseum.png

Fun Fact

> The Great Sphinx is 66 feet high and 241 feet long! It's carved of limestone. It is believed to be nearly 4,500 years old.

You can visit the Great Sphinx in Giza today. However, the Great Sphinx was not

> **Fun Fact**
> The Great Sphinx was buried up to its shoulders until the early 1800s. It was not completely unburied until the 1930s.

always visible. Much of it was buried in the sand for thousands of years.

Image of the Great Sphinx in 1849.
https://commons.wikimedia.org/wiki/File:Pyramids_%E2%80%94_Maxime_du_Camp.jpg

Between the front of the Great Sphinx rises an upright slab of granite rock with hieroglyphics carved into it. This stone is called the Dream **Stele** (*stee-lee*). The writing on this slab of rock tells the story of a young prince named **Thutmose**. He had a dream that the Sphinx told him to restore the statue. If he did so, the Sphinx promised that he would become pharaoh. Historians believe Pharaoh Thutmose IV built this stele.

The Dream Stele.
Chanel Wheeler, CC BY-SA 2.0 <https://creativecommons.org/licenses/by-sa/2.0>, via Wikimedia Commons; https://commons.wikimedia.org/wiki/File:Great_Sphinx_with_Stelae.jpg

The Great Pyramid at Giza is one of the Seven Wonders of the Ancient World. Over fourteen million people visit the three famous pyramids of Giza and the Great Sphinx every year.

> ## FUN FACT
> The Dream Stele is twelve feet tall and weighs fifteen tons! That's the combined weight of up to four hippos or two to three elephants!

The Giza pyramids.
KennyOMG, CC BY-SA 4.0 <https://creativecommons.org/licenses/by-sa/4.0>, via Wikimedia Commons; https://commons.wikimedia.org/wiki/File:Pyramids_of_the_Giza_Necropolis.jpg

Chapter 9 Activity

1. The Great Sphinx has the body of a _____.

2. The face of the Great Sphinx is believed to be that of _____.

3. The slab of rock found between the paws of the Sphinx is called the _____.

4. The Great Pyramid at Giza is known as one of the _____ wonders of the world.

5. The sphinx represents _____.

Chapter 9 Activity Answers

1. Lion
2. King Khafre
3. Dream Stele
4. 7 (seven)
5. Royal power, strength, or ferocity

Chapter 10: Of Gods and Humans

The ancient Egyptians believed in having a close relationship with their gods and goddesses. After all, the gods created everything in their world.

Their gods, goddesses, and myths helped them to understand the world around them. They also believed these gods kept balance in the world. For example, the gods brought darkness and day. Stories about the gods allowed the ancient Egyptians to know the difference between good and evil.

The world needed to have balance and laws. So, the people of ancient Egypt had pharaohs. These rulers were believed to be a very important link between mankind and the divine.

Image of woman worshiping Ra.
https://commons.wikimedia.org/wiki/File:Taperet_stele_E52_mp3h9201.jpg

The ancient Egyptians believed that because the pharaoh shared a special relationship with the gods, he was also divine. He was mortal, but he was connected in a unique way to the gods. The pharaohs encouraged harmony between mankind and the divine.

The rulers of Egypt were powerful. They were often feared by their subjects because of their close link to the gods. Yet the pharaohs had many duties. They held ceremonies to honor the gods. They kept the people safe from enemies. They made laws and collected taxes.

The pharaoh's main job was to make sure that the people maintained a sense of order so that the gods didn't grow angry with them. If there was disorder, the people would experience disharmony. Their crops wouldn't grow. The lands would be invaded by enemies. The people would starve and fall ill. By being "good," they made sure that their crops grew and that the kingdom stayed safe.

Ma'at required people to behave with truth and honor. The opposite of Ma'at was *Isfet*, or chaos, violence, and evil. Both needed to exist at the same time to maintain balance. The ancient Egyptians believed that if the pharaoh could maintain that balance, he was supported by the gods.

Sacred Places of the Gods

In ancient Egypt, many temples were built by the pharaohs to honor the gods and goddesses of ancient Egypt.

The remains of one of those temples, the Luxor Temple, can still be seen today. The temple is found on the east bank of the Nile River. It was built during the years of the New

Kingdom. The Luxor Temple was built to remember the kings. Many pharaohs added something to this temple, including Amenhotep III and Tutankhamun.

Image of the ruins of the Luxor Temple.
Ad Meskens, CC BY-SA 3.0 <https://creativecommons.org/licenses/by-sa/3.0>, via Wikimedia Commons; https://commons.wikimedia.org/wiki/File:Pylons_and_obelisk_Luxor_temple.JPG

During the Roman era, the Luxor Temple was dedicated to Mut, the goddess of the symbolic mother of the pharaoh.

Another sacred Egyptian symbol was the pointed stone that was placed on the very top of the pyramid or obelisk. It was known as the Benben stone. It was believed that the Benben stone symbolized the primeval mound from which all life arose. It was seen as a connection to the sun god Ra.

Reconstructed capstone symbolizing Benben at a pyramid in Giza.
Jon Bodsworth, Copyrighted free use, via Wikimedia Commons;
https://commons.wikimedia.org/wiki/File:Pyramidion-satellite-kh%C3%A9ops.jpg

Many temples were dedicated to Ra, the sun god. Many of them have been lost to history, but the remains of one can be seen in Heliopolis today. The obelisk of the Temple of Ra-Atum, built by Senusret (r. c. 1971–1926 BCE), can still be seen in Cairo today.

Today, visitors to Egypt can still see many ruins of temples, pyramids, and tombs. These structures, like the gods and goddesses, were very important to the people who lived in ancient times.

Obelisk at the Temple of Ra-Atum.
Roland Unger, CC BY-SA 3.0 <https://creativecommons.org/licenses/by-sa/3.0>,
via Wikimedia Commons; https://commons.wikimedia.org/wiki/File:CairoObeliskSesostris1.jpg

Conclusion

The myths of ancient Egypt had an effect on Egyptian beliefs, religion, and rituals. Egyptian society has left behind amazing proof of their dedication to their gods and goddesses, as well as their pharaohs.

If it were not for these pyramids, tombs, and statues, people today would know little of the lives of the ancient Egyptians. The gods and goddesses of those people are still commonly known today, thanks to movies, books, and Egyptian mythology.

Chapter 10 Activity

Decide which of the following statements are true and which are false.

1. The sacred symbol of the mound from which all life rose was called a sphinx.
2. Isfet was a word that meant balance.
3. The ancient Egyptians believed the gods kept the world in balance.
4. During the Roman era, the Luxor Temple was dedicated to Ra.
5. In ancient Egypt, the word Ma'at implied harmony and order.

Chapter 10 Activity Answers

1. False – It was Benben.
2. False – It means chaos.
3. True
4. False – It was dedicated to Mut.
5. True

Check out another book in the series

Click here to check out this book!

References

Gods and Myths of Ancient Egypt. Armour, Robert A. 2001. The American University of Cairo Press, Cairo.
Egyptian Mythology A to Z. Remler, Pat. 2000. Facts on File, Inc. New York, New York.
Understanding Egyptian Myths. Doyle, Sheri. 2012. Crabtree Publishing Company, New York.
Egyptian Mythology – Mythology and Culture Worldwide. Nardo, Don. Lucent Books. Cengage Learning, Michigan.
Egyptian Myths: Meet the Gods, Goddesses, and Pharaohs of Ancient Egypt. Menzies, Jean. 2022. DK Publishing. Penguin Random House. New York.
Egyptian Mythology. Nardo, Don. 2021. ReferencePoint Press, Inc. San Diego, CA.
Egyptian Myths. Retold by Morley, Jacqueline. 1999. Peter Bedrick Books. NTC/Contemporary Publishing Group.
Creation Myths and Form(s) of the gods in ancient Egypt: https://www.khanacademy.org/humanities/ancient-art-civilizations/egypt-art/beginners-guide-egypt/a/creation-myths-and-form-s-of-the-gods-in-ancient-egypt
Ancient Egyptian Mythology: https://www.worldhistory.org/Egyptian_Mythology/
Narmer: https://www.worldhistory.org/Narmer/
Ra: https://arce.org/resource/ra-creator-god-ancient-egypt/
Ra: https://www.worldhistory.org/Ra_(Egyptian_God)/
Balance & the Law in Ancient Egypt: https://www.worldhistory.org/article/1126/balance--the-law-in-ancient-egypt/
Book of the Heavenly Cow: https://www.worldhistory.org/Book_of_the_Heavenly_Cow/
Ogdoad of Hermopolis: https://ancientegyptonline.co.uk/ogdoad/
Ennead: http://globalegyptianmuseum.org/glossary.aspx?id=147
Ra – Book of Gates: https://ancientegyptonline.co.uk/bookgates/
Three Kingdoms of Ancient Egypt: https://www.ancient-egypt-online.com/ancient-egypt-kingdoms.html
Nun: https://www.britannica.com/topic/Nun-Egyptian-god
Egypt Exploration Society: Temples in Ancient Egypt: https://www.ees.ac.uk/temples-in-ancient-egypt
Rosicrucian Egyptian Museum: Deities in Ancient Egypt – Ma'at: https://egyptianmuseum.org/deities-Maat#:~:text=Ma'at%20was%20the%20goddess,she%20was%20depicted%20with%20wings.
Britannica: 11 Egyptian Gods and Goddesses: https://www.britannica.com/list/11-egyptian-gods-and-goddesses

www.ingramcontent.com/pod-product-compliance
Lightning Source LLC
Chambersburg PA
LSW072102050526
807CB00099B/383